WINDSOR CASTLE

OFFICIAL GUIDE

The most romantique castle in the world
SAMUEL PEPYS

CONTENTS

Windsor Castle is probably the best-known symbol of the British Monarchy. It is the only Royal residence which has been in continuous use since William the Conqueror chose the site for a fortress after his conquest of England in 1066.

This guide-book seeks to describe two things in particular: first, how the Castle is used today by The Queen and the rest of the Castle community (about 350 people); and second, the Castle's principal features, contents and history.

The Queen is often in residence in the Castle. During her visits the Royal Standard is flown from the flagpole above the Round Tower, while in her absence it is replaced by the Union Jack.

The State Apartments have been used by Sovereigns for some 900 years and contain many treasures from the Royal Collection. The magnificent St George's Chapel is the burial place of ten Sovereigns and the spiritual home of the Order of the Garter.

BELOW: *Windsor Castle, the north front from the Home Park, photographed by HRH The Duke of York.*

The area covered by the Castle is approximately 13 acres (5.26 hectares). The top of the Round Tower is 215 feet (65.5 m) above the level of the River Thames; and 280 feet (85.3 m) above sea level.

1	King Henry VIII Gate	28	King George IV Tower	53	Queen's Tower
2	Salisbury Tower	29	Grand Staircase (formerly Brick Court)	54	Sovereign's Entrance
3	Garter Tower			55	Grand Corridor
4	Curfew Tower	30	King's Dining Room	56	Augusta Tower
5	Guard Room	31	King's Drawing Room	57	York Tower
6	Horseshoe Cloister	32	King's State Bedchamber	58	King George IV Gate
7	St George's Chapel	33	King's Dressing Room	59	Lancaster Tower
8	Garter House	34	King's Closet	60	King Edward III Tower
9	Mary Tudor Tower	35	Queen's Drawing Room	61	St George's Gate
10	Albert Memorial Chapel	36	Queen's Ballroom	62	Exhibition of The Queen's Presents and Royal Carriages
11	Deanery	37	Queen's Audience Chamber		
12	Dean's Cloister	38	Queen's Presence Chamber		
13	Canons' Cloister	39	Queen's Guard Chamber		
14	Site of Inner Gatehouse	40	St George's Hall		
15	King Henry III Tower	41	Grand Reception Room		
16	Saxon Tower	42	Garter Throne Room		
17	Round Tower	43	Waterloo Chamber (formerly Horn Court)	S	Shop
18	Moat Garden				
19	Winchester Tower	44	Grand Vestibule	T	Toilet
20	Store Tower	45	King John's Tower		
21	Entrance to North Terrace	46	King Charles II Statue		
22	Magazine Tower	47	The Moat Path		
23	Norman Gate	48	State Entrance		
24	Engine Court	49	Brunswick Tower		
25	Steps to North Terrace	50	Prince of Wales's Tower		
26	Entrance to State Apartments	51	Chester Tower		
27	Entrance to Dolls' House	52	Clarence Tower		

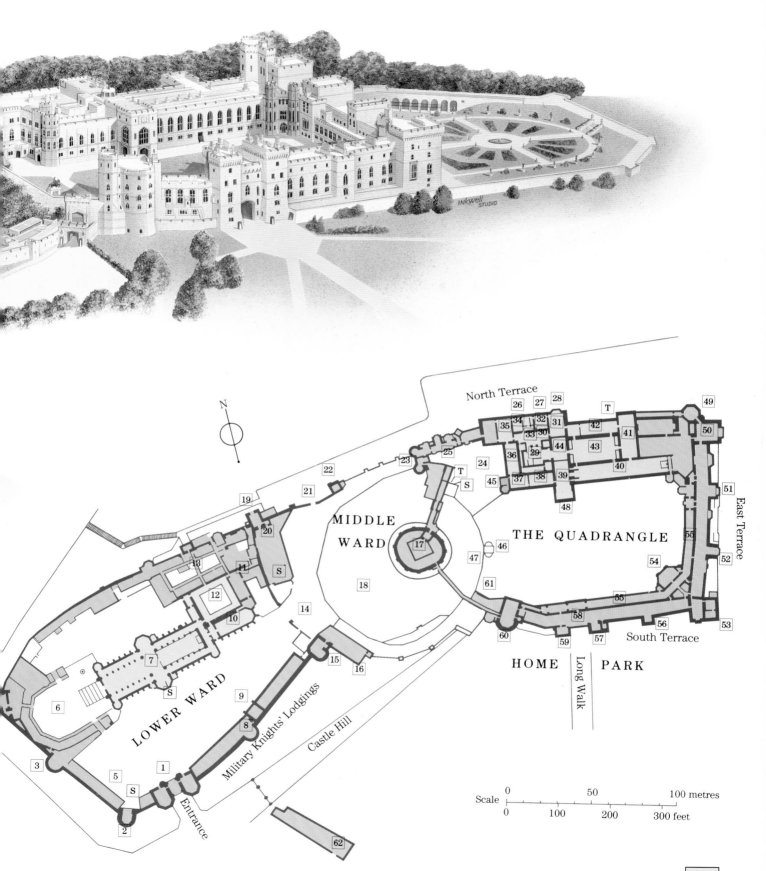

North Terrace

MIDDLE WARD

THE QUADRANGLE

LOWER WARD

Military Knights' Lodgings

Castle Hill

Entrance

East Terrace

South Terrace

HOME PARK

Long Walk

N

Scale	0	50	100 metres
	0	100	200	300 feet

The main entrance to Windsor Castle is through the King Henry VIII Gate built in 1511. An armorial panel above the arch is carved with the Tudor rose of Henry VIII and the pomegranate of his first wife, Catherine of Aragon. The gateway used to have a portcullis, the grooves of which are visible on each side.

To repel assailants boiling oil could be poured by the defenders through the holes visible in the arch. Formerly a ditch ran in front of the gateway, crossed by a drawbridge which was removed in the 1670s.

Passing through the gateway into the Lower Ward, the visitor sees, straight ahead, St George's Chapel. On the left are the Lower Ward shop, the Salisbury Tower (residence of a member of the Royal Household), the Guard Room, and, stretching across to St George's Chapel, the backs of houses forming the Horseshoe Cloister. On the right, flanking the outer wall, are the residences of the Military Knights.

Each year, in June, The Queen, wearing the robes of the Order of the Garter, Britain's highest Order of Chivalry, processes down this hill with the other Knights of the Garter into St George's Chapel for their annual service. After the service Her Majesty and other members of the Royal Family drive back up the hill in horse-drawn carriages.

The Guard Room houses the soldiers who are always on guard duty within the Castle. In the winter months the ceremony of the

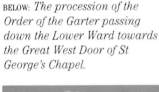

BELOW: *The procession of the Order of the Garter passing down the Lower Ward towards the Great West Door of St George's Chapel.*

Changing of the Guard takes place in front of the Guard Room. The building is of recent date (1862) compared with the outer west wall of the Castle (1220s) against which it stands. An archway leads through to the Horseshoe Cloister.

The houses in the cloister are occupied by members of the staff of St George's Chapel, including the Lay Clerks (Choirmen) who, together with the boy choristers who are educated in the choir school below the north-west wall of the Castle, sing in St George's Chapel Choir. The cloister was originally built in 1478–81 by King Edward IV, founder of the present St George's Chapel, for the priest-vicars who served in the Chapel. It was restored in 1871 and again in 1952.

LEFT: *Soldiers marching out of the King Henry VIII Gate after the Changing of the Guard.*

RIGHT: *King Henry VIII Gate in about 1780. A watercolour by Paul Sandby.*

BELOW: *The Lower Ward of the Castle with St George's Chapel on the left, the Round Tower, the lodgings of the Military Knights of Windsor and the inside of Henry VIII Gate.*

ABOVE: *The Curfew Tower dates from the 1220s with alterations to its roof and outer wall in 1863. It houses the eight bells of St George's Chapel. The dungeon is open to school groups visiting the Chapel by arrangement.*

Opposite the cloister is the Great West Door of St George's Chapel, through which The Queen enters and leaves the Chapel during the formal services she attends.

The Curfew Tower is reached from the far side of the Horseshoe Cloister. The conical roof was added in 1863, as was the stone facing on the street side. But the inside of the tower retains much of its original medieval structure dating from the 1220s, when it was built by King Henry III. The dungeon in the basement retains its 13th-century vaulting and its 13-foot (3.9 m) thick walls. The clock in the tower was made in Windsor in 1689. The tower also contains the eight bells of St George's Chapel, which were moved here in 1477.

Through the farther archway of Horseshoe Cloister, the visitor can reach the Library Terrace or Lookout, which gives an excellent view to the north. On the right is a series of buildings which belong to the Dean and Canons of St George's Chapel.

RIGHT: *The roof of St George's Chapel, looking west. The stone figures are heraldic beasts, the emblems of 15th-century monarchs. They were originally erected in 1557 but were renewed in 1930.*

ABOVE AND FAR RIGHT: *Lion and unicorn at the bottom of the St George's Chapel West Steps, carved 1920–30, bearing the Royal Arms as at 1837. The steps were built in 1872 and renewed in 1981.*

RIGHT: *The Queen leaving St George's Chapel by the Great West Door after the annual service of the Order of the Garter. The Queen is accompanied by Queen Elizabeth The Queen Mother and The Prince of Wales.*

RIGHT: *Sunday morning in the Lower Ward in 1840. The choir emerges from the Horseshoe Cloister on its way to morning service. A military band plays on the grass (right). A watercolour by Joseph Nash.*

St George's Chapel is revered among Royal shrines for its association with the Order of the Garter, Britain's highest Order of Chivalry, founded by King Edward III in 1348. St George is the patron saint of the Order. Today the 13 Military Knights of Windsor represent the Knights of the Garter in St George's Chapel. Ten Sovereigns are buried in the Chapel.

The building of the Chapel was begun by King Edward IV in 1475. By 1484 the Choir was finished, roofed in wood. His son-in-law, King Henry VII, completed the nave and added the stone-vaulted ceiling throughout before his death in 1509. King Henry VIII completed the building by 1528.

The architecture of the Chapel ranks among the finest examples of the Perpendicular Gothic, the late medieval style of English architecture. Unlike most other great churches, St George's has its principal or 'show' front on the south, facing the visitor entering by the Henry VIII Gate.

St George's Chapel has a very busy life today. The Dean, four Canons and the rest of their staff undertake many activities from the regular round of daily prayers to the numerous special services and Royal occasions.

As Sovereign of the Order of the Garter, The Queen, in June each year, attends a service in the Chapel with the Knights and Ladies of the Order.

ABOVE: *The back of a stall belonging to a Knight of the Garter. To it are attached enamelled plates, each displaying the arms of a Knight. The earliest shield dates from the 14th century.*

RIGHT: *The Nave, described as 'the culmination of the English late Gothic style'. The organ screen, though Gothic in style, was designed in the late 18th century by Henry Emlyn. The organ was rebuilt in the 1930s.*

ABOVE: *The East Doorway was once the Great West Door of Henry III's Chapel, built in 1240–48. The original 13th-century ironwork by Gilbertus was gilded in 1955.*

RIGHT: *The Choir of the Chapel. Above the beautifully carved stalls (1478–95) hang the banners of each Knight of the Garter with his helmet and crest below. The East Window (1863) was inserted in memory of Prince Albert.*

LEFT: *The south windows with stained glass depicting ancestors of Prince Albert. The mosaics on the ceiling are Venetian glass. The marble inlay work on the walls was designed by Baron Triqueti.*

The richly decorated interior of the Albert Memorial Chapel was created by Sir George Gilbert Scott for Queen Victoria in 1863–73 to commemorate her husband Albert, the Prince Consort, who died in 1861 at the early age of 42. The vaulted ceiling is decorated in Venetian glass mosaic by Antonio Salviati. The figures in the false West Window represent Sovereigns, clerics and others associated with St George's Chapel. The illustrated marble panels around the walls depict scenes from Scripture.

This was the site of one of the Castle's earliest chapels, built in 1240 by King Henry III and adapted by King Edward III in the 1350s as the first chapel of the College of St George and the Order of the Garter. When the existing St George's Chapel was built between 1475 and 1528, this small chapel fell into disuse. Subsequent plans to turn it into a Royal mausoleum came to nothing.

In 1863 Queen Victoria ordered its complete restoration and redecoration as a temporary resting place for Prince Albert. Prince Albert's tomb was later moved to the Royal Mausoleum at Frogmore. The Chapel is now dominated by Alfred Gilbert's tomb of the Duke of Clarence and Avondale (elder son of King Edward VII) who died in 1892. (*Public access only by special arrangement.*)

BELOW LEFT: *Detail from the white marble effigy of Prince Albert in fluted armour.*

BELOW: *The Chapel looking west. The West Window is blocked with mosaic pictures of persons associated with St George's Chapel.*

The Middle Ward is dominated by the might of the Round Tower, the central feature of Windsor Castle, bearing the Royal Standard when The Queen is in residence and the Union Jack at other times. The Round Tower is flanked on the north by the Norman Tower and Gateway. On the right is the King Henry III Tower with Saxon Tower beyond; on the left, Winchester Tower and Store Tower.

ABOVE: *The Norman Tower and Gate dating from 1359–60. The room above the gateway was used as a prison. The Governor of the Castle lives in the tower.*

BELOW RIGHT: *The Queen and Prince Philip in the robes of the Order of the Garter processing to the annual service of the Order in St George's Chapel.*

The King Henry III Tower, which was built in the 1220s, houses members of the Royal Household. The two distinctive round-headed windows, inserted by Hugh May in the 1670s, are the only two which remain in the Castle, the others having all been replaced by windows in the Gothic style. The Saxon Tower is used as offices by the administrative staff of the Castle.

Opposite and north of the King Henry III Tower is the office of the Castle Superintendent, who is in charge of the day-to-day administration of the Castle, and next to that are Store Tower and Winchester Tower, occupied by members of the Royal Household. Winchester Tower was built in the 1170s by King Henry II but rebuilt in 1357–58 when William of Wykeham, Clerk of Works to King Edward III, lived there. King George IV's architect, Sir Jeffry Wyatville, occupied the tower from 1824 until his death in 1840.

The wall which runs from Winchester Tower to the Norman Gate was built in the 1170s. It is pierced by a gateway which leads to the North Terrace. The small Magazine Tower half way along the wall was built in 1457.

The Round Tower houses the Royal Archives and the Royal Photograph Collection. Before the Archives were installed in the tower in 1911, it had been occupied at varying times by the Governor of the Castle or by members of the Royal Household. King Edward III himself lived in it for several years in the 1360s when his private apartments in the Upper Ward were being altered.

RIGHT: *The Round Tower with the Royal Standard flying, indicating that The Queen is in residence.*

BELOW: *The Moat Garden below the Round Tower is the private garden of the Governor of the Castle. It has never held water as its chalk base is porous.*

The original Round Tower was built of wood by King William I in the 1070s. In the 1170s the lower half of the existing stone structure was erected by King Henry II. In the 1820s King George IV had the Tower heightened by 30 feet (9.1 m).

The Norman Tower and the Norman Gate are at the foot of the Round Tower on the north side. The Norman Tower is the residence of the Governor of the Castle, who has overall responsibility for Windsor Castle in The Queen's absence. The post is usually held by a retired senior officer of the armed services. The gateway, dating in its present form from 1359–60, guarded the Upper Ward where the Sovereigns had, as today, their Private Apartments.

As in the case of the King Henry VIII Gate, the Norman Gate is fitted with a portcullis and the arch above is pierced with vents for the purpose of defence. The room above this arch was formerly used as a prison. Its most notable prisoners were King John of France, King David of Scotland, and a later King of Scotland, King James I, who spent 11 years in captivity in the Castle.

The Moat Garden is the Governor's private garden (*open to the public on a few afternoons each summer*). The Moat was dug in the 1070s, its spoil being used to make the mound on which the Round Tower stands. The zig-zag lines on the mound indicate drainage channels.

ABOVE: *Saxon Tower and the back of King Henry III Tower looking west.*

The Quadrangle forms the impressive centrepiece of the Upper Ward, where Sovereigns have had their private living quarters for over 900 years. It provides the setting for a number of colourful ceremonies of state, presided over by the handsome equestrian statue of King Charles II beneath the Round Tower.

ABOVE: *Equestrian statue of King Charles II (1660–85), first erected in 1680 in the centre of the Quadrangle and moved to its present position in the 1820s.*

BELOW: *A foreign Head of State visiting The Queen arrives by horse-drawn carriage escorted by the Household Cavalry.*

On passing through the Norman Gate, the visitor enters Engine Court, so named because of the engine which pumped water up into the Castle from 1677. In the building on the left, which was erected in 1583 by Queen Elizabeth I, the principal apartment is a gallery on the first floor which the Queen used for taking exercise in the winter. The next section on the left, up to the Side Door, was built by King Henry VII in the 1480s. These rooms now contain the Royal Library (*not open to the public*). Her Majesty Queen Elizabeth II regularly shows her guests around the Library after dinner.

The Quadrangle of the Upper Ward is surrounded on the left (north) by the State Apartments (*open to the public when The Queen is not in official residence*), and on the east and south by the Private Apartments (*not open to the public*), where Her Majesty, her family and guests reside.

The Quadrangle is the setting for a number of colourful ceremonies. When a foreign Head of State pays a State Visit, he is received in the Home Park by The Queen, who accompanies him in a horse-drawn carriage procession through the town, up the Long Walk and through the King George IV Gate into the Quadrangle. Here he takes the salute at a rank past of the Royal Horse Artillery, followed by the Sovereign's Escort of the Household Cavalry and a march past of the Guard of Honour.

RIGHT: *The Upper Ward before (below) and after (above) King George IV's architect Sir Jeffry Wyatville altered it in the 1820s.*

BELOW RIGHT: *Guard changing next to the State Entrance, built in the 1820s.*

BELOW FAR RIGHT: *Queen Elizabeth I's Gallery (left) and King Henry VII's rooms (right) now form the Royal Library.*

RIGHT: *The North Terrace looking east. The left tower is the west end of the gallery built by Queen Elizabeth I in 1583. Watercolour by Paul Sandby.*

ABOVE: *The North Terrace looking east today. The left tower is now part of the Royal Library.*

When Her Majesty is in official residence, the Changing of the Guard takes place in the Quadrangle. Other ceremonies, such as the review of senior Scouts, are also held here.

In the south-east corner of the Quadrangle is the Sovereign's Entrance, through which personal guests of The Queen enter the Castle. At first floor level, along the entire length of the east and south fronts, runs the Grand Corridor. Most of these features were added by King George IV's architect, Sir Jeffry Wyatville, in the 1820s. He also moved the equestrian statue of King Charles II from the centre of the Quadrangle to its present position at the foot of the Round Tower.

It was King George IV and Wyatville who were primarily responsible for making the Upper Ward look as it does today, by adding numerous and elaborate castellations and turrets, raising the height of the Queen's Tower (south-east corner of the Upper Ward) and York Tower (left of the King George IV Gate), building a new tower (Lancaster Tower) to match York Tower, creating the King George IV Gate as well as St George's Gate (south-west corner) and heightening the east and south sides of the Private Apartments to provide more staff quarters.

The North Terrace (*reached from Engine Court by steps under Queen Elizabeth I's Gallery*) runs along the entire length of the Upper and Middle Wards and gives an excellent view over the Thames and Eton and on to Slough and the Chiltern Hills. The diarist John Evelyn described it in 1645 as 'one of the most delightful prospects in the world.' It also shows why the Castle was built where it is, on a bluff overlooking the river and the western approach to London.

The East Terrace Garden can be seen from the eastern part of the North Terrace. The private garden was laid out for King George IV by Sir Jeffry Wyatville in the 1820s. The garden is open to the public on some Sunday afternoons in the summer when a military band plays on the East Terrace under the windows of the Private Apartments.

ABOVE: *The East Terrace Garden today. The garden was created by King George IV in the 1820s.*

LEFT: *The East Terrace Garden in the 1840s. Watercolour by Joseph Nash.*

RIGHT: *The Borghese gladiator, by Hubert Le Sueur, was cast in bronze for King Charles I. The statue was brought to the newly-created East Terrace Garden by King George IV.*

'We went over to the State Rooms which are ever a fresh entertainment to look at' wrote Queen Victoria in her Journal of 14 August 1841. The State Apartments were so named because they constitute the grand parade rooms used principally on ceremonial occasions. In the 19th century visiting Heads of State were lodged in these apartments. In the present reign The Queen continues to use them to entertain such visitors.

ABOVE: *King Henry VIII's suit of armour, made in about 1540 in the armouries at Greenwich.*

In recent years the King of Norway, the Presidents of Poland and Malawi and the Sheikh of Bahrain have paid State Visits to The Queen at Windsor Castle.

From the 1070s to the late 17th century both the Private and State Apartments were in this area of the Castle, and were occupied by successive Kings and Queens and their families. King Henry II (1154–89) and King Henry III (1216–72) erected sturdy stone buildings, to which additions were made by King Edward III (1327–77).

King Charles II (1660–85) largely rebuilt these apartments in the 1670s. He employed the architect Hugh May, the Italian artist Antonio Verrio and the famous wood-carver Grinling Gibbons to create a lavish series of rooms in the baroque style. The King's apartments faced north and the Queen had the sunnier rooms looking south into the Quadrangle.

During much of the 18th century the Castle was rarely visited by the Sovereign. The transformations which were later carried out, initiated by King George IV, were completed for the most part in the 1830s during the succeeding reign of King William IV. The State Apartments contain some of the finest paintings and works of art in the Royal Collection.

The Grand Staircase, which is on the site of a medieval herb garden (later known as Brick Court), was built for Queen Victoria in 1866–67 by the architect Anthony Salvin. It replaced an earlier staircase on this site dating from the 1820s, which Sir Jeffry Wyatville had erected for King George IV. Dominating the stairwell is the statue of King George IV by Sir Francis Chantrey, which was completed in 1830.

RIGHT: *Ice pail from the Rockingham porcelain service; commissioned by King William IV in 1830 and first used at the Coronation of Queen Victoria in 1838.*

LEFT: *Fruit basket from the Worcester porcelain service; commissioned by William IV in 1830. It is still used by The Queen on formal occasions at Windsor Castle.*

RIGHT: *The Grand Staircase. An open courtyard till the 1820s, it is now dominated by the statue of King George IV, who made many changes to the Castle.*

King Charles II's Dining Room is, of all the rooms in the State Apartments, the one which retains most of its 17th-century character. Its ceiling, by Antonio Verrio, depicts a banquet of the gods and the coving has fish and fruit hung in garlands. They echo the spectacular carvings in limewood by Grinling Gibbons and others, composed of garlands of flowers and fruit and swags of dead game.

A spirited terracotta bust of King Charles II is turned towards the portrait of his wife, Queen Catherine of Braganza, depicted as a shepherdess, by Jacob Huysmans, which hangs over the chimney-piece.

The pair of mirrors (originally picture frames) facing across the entrance bear the initials of King William III and Queen Mary II and were made in England in the 1690s. In the window alcove to the left of the entrance is an ornate pair of bellows with silver mounts which King Charles II is said to have given to his friend Nell Gwynn, for whom he built a house close to the Castle. The windows used to look into an open courtyard, Brick Court.

Facing across the fireplace are early 18th-century English mirrors with the cypher of Queen Anne. The two panels of tapestry are Brussels, *c.* 1690 and display the arms of King William III. Below the left-hand tapestry is a Boulle secretaire, French 18th-century, in the Louis XIV style. It was bought by King George IV for Carlton House, the King's London residence.

On the left of the exit is a picture by Sir Godfrey Kneller entitled *The Chinese Convert*. Opposite is an unusual portrait by John Riley of a chambermaid, Bridget Holmes, who between the 1640s and the 1690s served four kings, Charles I, Charles II, James II and William III, and lived to be over 100.

LEFT: *The King's Dining Room. The decoration of the room has been altered in several respects since King Charles II had it made in the 1670s.*

RIGHT: *Louis XIV-style Boulle secretaire, bought by King George IV, originally for Carlton House.*

FAR RIGHT: *A late 17th-century French clock bought by King George IV in 1820. The Boulle and tortoise-shell case is mounted in ormolu. The clock was brought to Windsor Castle in 1835.*

King Charles II could withdraw into this room either from his Dining Room or from his Audience Chamber, which was through the doors opposite the fireplace. The window bay was an addition commissioned by King George IV in 1829. The ceiling, which bears George IV's cypher, the Royal Arms and the Garter Star, dates from this period.

It was in this room that the body of King George IV lay in state after his death in 1830. In Queen Victoria's reign the room was sometimes used for theatricals, a stage being erected in the window bay. It was here, for example, that in 1848 Charles Kean's company performed Shakespeare's *The Merchant of Venice* for the Queen.

Since the late 18th century this room has also been known as the Rubens Room. Three paintings by this artist still hang here. They were bought by King George III's father, Frederick, Prince of Wales, and represent the Holy Family (*above the chimney-piece*) flanked by a summer landscape and a winter scene. The equestrian portrait (*opposite door from Dining Room*) of King Philip II of Spain, who married Queen Mary I of England in 1554, is after Rubens, as is also the portrait of a bare-headed equestrian figure in armour (*opposite window*).

ABOVE: *Clock made by John Pyke, London (1720–62), in an English case lacquered in the Italian style. It was bought by The Queen in 1960.*

BELOW RIGHT: *Queen Victoria and Prince Albert watching a performance of* Macbeth *in the King's Drawing Room in 1853.*

RIGHT: *The King's Drawing Room. It was sometimes called the Rubens room because the majority of the paintings were by this artist.*

LEFT: *The Queen showing her guests a Rubens painting in this room. Guests include ambassadors, politicians, industrialists and, on this occasion, Margaret Thatcher and the Poet Laureate.*

Although King Charles II did not use this room as his bedroom, notwithstanding its stated function, it was used by the King as a closet to which only ministers of state and other advisers were admitted. It was here that he transacted much of his business.

ABOVE: *Colonel John St Leger (1782) by Thomas Gainsborough. Commissioned by King George IV when Prince of Wales. St Leger was a close friend.*

LEFT: *The King's State Bedchamber. The State Bed is French, late 18th-century. It was decorated for the visit of Napoleon III to Windsor in 1855.*

In the 19th century it served as a bedroom for State Visits. In 1855, for example, it was occupied by the Empress Eugénie, who slept in the 18th-century French four-poster bed. The cyphers at the foot of the bed, LN and EI (for Louis Napoleon and Eugénie *Imperatores*), were embroidered in honour of that occasion.

The chimney-piece, which is of 18th-century date and was originally in Buckingham House, was probably moved to this room in the 1830s. At the same time the ceiling was renewed and the cypher of King Charles II reproduced in the corners.

The early 19th-century carpet was given to The Queen by President de Gaulle during his State Visit to England in 1960. The two inlaid English chests of drawers flanking the chimney-piece are attributed to Pierre Langlois, a London cabinet-maker of French extraction active in the third quarter of the 18th century.

Above them hang four views of Venice by Canaletto. These form part of the important purchase made by King George III in 1762 from Joseph Smith, British Consul in Venice, of some 50 paintings and 140 drawings by this artist. The two full-length portraits are by Gainsborough. The one over the chimney-piece is of the artist's son-in-law, the musician J. C. Fischer, who was a celebrated oboist and member of Queen Charlotte's band. The other is of Colonel John St Leger who was a boon companion of the Prince of Wales (the future King George IV). A closely-related painting, a portrait of the Prince of Wales, was presented to Colonel St Leger by the Prince and is now at Waddesdon Manor, in Buckinghamshire.

ABOVE: *The initials of King Charles II who originally made this into his bedchamber in the 1670s. The present ceiling was remade in the 1830s.*

BELOW CENTRE: *The King's State Bedchamber in 1855 for the visit of Napoleon III and the Empress Eugénie. Watercolour by W. Corden.*

In King Charles II's time this room was larger. Although the previous room was the King's State Bedroom, it was here that he slept. The changes initiated by King George IV left this room much reduced in size. Work was not completed until the following reign. The room contains some of the finest pictures in the Royal Collection.

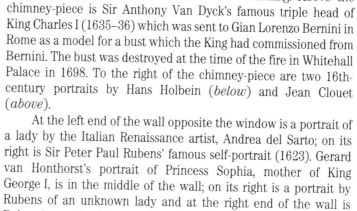

To the left of the chimney-piece, next to the entrance, are portraits by Albrecht Dürer and Hans Memling. Above the chimney-piece is Sir Anthony Van Dyck's famous triple head of King Charles I (1635–36) which was sent to Gian Lorenzo Bernini in Rome as a model for a bust which the King had commissioned from Bernini. The bust was destroyed at the time of the fire in Whitehall Palace in 1698. To the right of the chimney-piece are two 16th-century portraits by Hans Holbein (*below*) and Jean Clouet (*above*).

At the left end of the wall opposite the window is a portrait of a lady by the Italian Renaissance artist, Andrea del Sarto; on its right is Sir Peter Paul Rubens' famous self-portrait (1623). Gerard van Honthorst's portrait of Princess Sophia, mother of King George I, is in the middle of the wall; on its right is a portrait by Rubens of an unknown lady and at the right end of the wall is Rubens' portrait of Van Dyck (1628).

On the left of the exit is Rembrandt's portrait of an elderly woman, possibly his mother (*c.* 1629), next to which is Van Dyck's

TOP: *Rembrandt's portrait of a young man in a turban (1631).*

ABOVE: *Rubens' self-portrait (1623).*

RIGHT: *The portrait of King Charles I (1635–6) by Sir Anthony Van Dyck, which was specially commissioned to send to Rome to enable the sculptor Bernini to make a bust.*

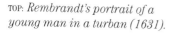
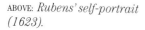

ABOVE LEFT: *Portrait of a young man by Albrecht Dürer (1471–1528). Bought by King Charles I for the Royal Collection.*

ABOVE: *Queen Henrietta Maria, wife of King Charles I, by Sir Anthony Van Dyck (1632).*

RIGHT: *The King's Dressing Room, which King Charles II used as his bedroom.*

portrait of Queen Henrietta Maria, wife of King Charles I (1632). Beyond that is another Rembrandt, a portrait of a young man in a turban.

In the centre of the wall opposite the window is a writing-desk veneered with Boulle marquetry of tortoise-shell, brass, pewter and stained horn and inlaid with the arms of the de Retz family. It is French and dates from the second half of the 17th century. The other desk is English, *c.* 1695, veneered with marquetry of brass and pewter and made by Gerrit Jensen for King William III. The King's and Queen Mary II's interlaced monogram is incorporated into the decoration.

This room was used by King Charles II as a private study. It was extensively altered in the 1830s. Incorporated in the design of the ceiling are the date 1833 and the name of Queen Adelaide, wife of King William IV.

The room, which was used as a bedroom in the 19th century, was occupied by Napoleon III and the Empress Eugénie in 1855 during their State Visit.

The paintings date from the 18th century. Canaletto's painting of Venice (*on the wall opposite the window*) forms part of the important purchase made by King George III in 1762 from Joseph Smith, British Consul in Venice, of some 50 paintings and 140 drawings by this artist. Opposite the chimney-piece is a full-length portrait by Sir Joshua Reynolds of the Marquis of Hastings, a friend of King George IV, flanked on the right by Allan Ramsay's portrait of Queen Charlotte's brother, George Augustus of Mecklenburg-Strelitz, and on the left by the youthful portrait of the future King William IV which is also by Ramsay. Over the chimney-piece hangs Hogarth's portrait of the celebrated 18th-century actor, David Garrick, and his wife, and to its right another of the same sitter, as portrayed by Reynolds. To the left of the chimney is a painting by Richard Brompton of King George III's brother, Edward Duke of York, on the Grand Tour in Italy.

The set of mahogany seats (1780s) are French but in the English style. The chimney-piece came from Queen Charlotte's Japanned Room in Buckingham House in the 1830s.

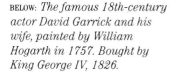

BELOW: *The famous 18th-century actor David Garrick and his wife, painted by William Hogarth in 1757. Bought by King George IV, 1826.*

BELOW: *This lacquer chest of drawers and the corner cupboards are French, mid 18th-century, by Bernard [II] Van Risamburgh.*

RIGHT: *The King's Closet was used by King Charles II as a private study. King William IV altered it in the 1830s; his wife's name, Adelaide, appears in the ceiling design.*

The visitor now passes from the apartments originally occupied by King Charles II to those occupied by his consort, Queen Catherine of Braganza. Her Drawing Room, together with her four succeeding rooms (Ballroom, Audience, Presence and Guard Chambers) formed part of the Star Building erected for King Charles II in 1675–78.

ABOVE: *A painting by Hans Holbein of Sir Henry Guildford (1527), Comptroller of the Household of King Henry VIII.*

BELOW CENTRE: *The Queen regularly shows her dinner guests through these rooms. Her Majesty is seen here with a Bishop and an African High Commissioner.*

The door opposite the entrance led directly into the Queen's State Bedroom, which is now occupied by the Royal Library (*not open to the public*). To the left of the exit a door leads into the Dining Room used by King Charles II and Queen Catherine.

In the early 1830s Antonio Verrio's ceiling was replaced by the existing one, which incorporates the cyphers of King William IV and Queen Adelaide and the date 1834. The chimney-piece must also have been inserted at this time. Between 1840 and 1963 this room was called the Picture Gallery.

Today it is hung with portraits of Tudor and Stuart monarchs. To the left of the fireplace are portraits by or after Hans Holbein, including King Henry VIII, his Lord Chamberlain the Duke of Norfolk (*c.* 1538–39), and a German merchant Derich Born (1533). To the right of the fireplace are paintings of King Henry VIII's three children, King Edward VI (1547–53), Queen Mary I (1553–58) and Queen Elizabeth I (1558–1603).

On the left and right of the exit are the state portrait of King James I by Paul van Somer (*c.* 1620) and a portrait of his son King Charles I by Daniel Mytens (1628). King James's elder son, Henry, Prince of Wales, who predeceased his father in 1612, is represented in the hunting field in a painting over the chimney-piece.

Opposite the fireplace is an elaborately carved ebony-veneered cabinet. It is French and dates from the mid-17th century. Above it is a view of Windsor Castle from the north by Leonard Knyff dating from 1701, and to the right Sir Peter Lely's allegorical portrait of Mary II when Princess of Orange, who is represented in the role of Diana, goddess of hunting.

ABOVE: *Princess Elizabeth (the future Queen Elizabeth I) aged about 13. Artist unknown.*

RIGHT: *The Queen's Drawing Room, made by King Charles II for his Queen, Catherine of Braganza. The room was altered in the 1830s.*

ABOVE: *The Queen's Ballroom, made by King Charles II in the 1670s for Queen Catherine of Braganza. The room was further remodelled in the 1830s.*

RIGHT: *Detail from Sir Anthony Van Dyck's painting of the five eldest children of King Charles I. The future King Charles II is in the centre.*

It is in The Queen's Ballroom that visiting Heads of State receive members of the Diplomatic Corps on the occasion of State Visits. This and the next two rooms form part of the building erected in the 14th century by King Edward III to serve as a nursery wing. This room was remodelled in the 1670s for use by Queen Catherine of Braganza as her ballroom.

It remained the principal ballroom in the Castle up to the early 1830s when King George IV's Ballroom and the Waterloo Chamber came into use. When it was remodelled again in the 1830s, it was stripped of its panelling and painted ceiling and acquired a chimney-piece from the Queen's State Bedroom (now part of the Library).

In recent times the paintings by Sir Anthony Van Dyck were returned to this room, thus recreating a 19th-century arrangement, which may have first been planned by King George IV.

On the left as you enter the room is Van Dyck's impressive state portrait of King Charles I (1636), which remained the model for English Royal portraits up to the middle of the 18th century. To the left of the exit is Van Dyck's well-known portrait of the five eldest children of King Charles I (1637). The three children on the left are Princess Mary (mother of King William III), the future King James II and King Charles II (with his hand on the mastiff).

Between the windows are two silver tables and mirrors, which were presented by the citizens of London. The first set, dating from about 1700, was given to King William III, whose arms are engraved on the top of the table; and the second, which is accompanied by a pair of candle-stands, was a gift to King Charles II and dates from about 1660. Also on the window wall is a pair of English cabinets, *c.* 1665, veneered with oyster-cut *lignum vitae* and fitted with silver mounts. They probably belonged to Queen Henrietta Maria, wife of King Charles I.

ABOVE: *Negress head clock, French, late 18th century. If the right earring is pulled the time shows in the eye sockets; hours on the left, minutes on the right.*

BELOW RIGHT: *The top of the silver table (c. 1700) engraved with the arms of King William III, to whom it was given by the citizens of London.*

BELOW: *The Queen's Ballroom in the 1840s. Also referred to as the Van Dyck room, as it was entirely hung then, as now, with paintings by Van Dyck.*

By the late 17th century this room had become the Queen's main audience room. The principal furnishings consisted of a throne chair on a dais, set against a cloth of estate surmounted by a canopy.

Of the thirteen ceilings painted by the Italian artist Antonio Verrio in the State Apartments for King Charles II in the 1670s, only three survive. Here Queen Catherine of Braganza, wife of Charles II, is represented as Britannia, being driven in a triumphal carriage drawn by swans towards the Temple of Virtue.

Over the entrance is a portrait by Gerard van Honthorst of William II, Prince of Orange, husband of King Charles I's eldest daughter Mary, and father of King William III of England. The other painting, also by Honthorst, is of Frederick Henry, Prince of Orange, father of William II. Over the exit is a painting of Mary Queen of Scots, with an inset showing the scene of her execution at Fotheringay Castle in 1587.

The tapestries in this and the next room were woven in the Gobelins factory in France between 1779 and 1785, and were bought by King George IV in 1825. They form a series of seven scenes from the Old Testament Book of Esther. Because of their size they are not in strict order. They represent (*from right to left*) Esther selected as Queen; the humiliation of Haman, who is forced to lead the triumphant Mordecai (Esther's adopted father) through the streets on the King's horse; Esther purifying herself before being chosen as King Ahasuerus' second wife.

The other furnishings include a set of gilt gesso English chairs in the manner of William Kent which date from the 1730s and two 17th-century Flemish cabinets, one veneered with ebony, the other with ebony and tortoise-shell. On either side of the chimney-piece is an oriental lacquer cabinet on an English wood stand *c.* 1730. On the tables by the windows are two pairs of Japanese porcelain vases from the first half of the 18th century.

ABOVE: *Mary Queen of Scots (1542–87) by an unknown artist. Beneath the Queen's right hand is a representation of her execution at Fotheringay Castle in February 1587.*

RIGHT: *The Queen's Audience Chamber, made by King Charles II in the 1670s for his Queen, Catherine of Braganza. A throne would have stood in this room.*

ABOVE: *A Chinese porcelain vase, c. 1690–1710. Moved from Buckingham Palace to this room in 1927.*

RIGHT: *The ceiling painting is by Antonio Verrio, commissioned by King Charles II in the 1670s. Queen Catherine of Braganza is being drawn in a triumphal carriage.*

The Queen's Presence Chamber is now used as a robing room by the Knights of the Garter on Garter Day. This is the last of the three rooms retaining the main features of the apartments as remodelled for King Charles II: Verrio's painted ceiling, and the cornice and garlands carved by Grinling Gibbons and others. It was the principal audience room of his Queen, Catherine of Braganza. Subsequently it became a waiting room where the Page of the Presence prepared to take the visitor through to the previous room for an audience.

ABOVE: *Frances Stuart, Duchess of Richmond and Lennox, after a painting by Sir Peter Lely. The Duchess was a friend of King Charles II.*

LEFT: *The Queen's Presence Chamber. Its painted ceiling is by Antonio Verrio and forms part of the transformations of the Castle carried out for King Charles II in the 1670s.*

This room, like the previous one, retains its 17th-century wood-carvings and painted ceiling in which Queen Catherine is represented seated under a canopy as the figures of Envy and Sedition retreat before the outstretched sword of Justice. Also of 17th-century date is the panelling and the rich carving around the pictures and the coving. The chimney-piece, which was designed by Robert Adam for Queen Charlotte's Saloon at Buckingham House and is dated 1789, was moved to this room in the 1830s.

The Gobelins tapestries complete the set from the previous room. They show (*from left to right*): Haman arrested in the Queen's room; Mordecai alone refusing to bow the knee to Haman; Esther begging for the life of her people; Queen Esther asking her husband King Ahasuerus during a banquet not to carry out the plan of his adviser Haman to destroy the Jews.

The marble bust by the entrance door is of the composer George Frederick Handel (1739) by Roubiliac. Handel's music was particularly admired by King George III and was often played to the King in these apartments. The bust in the near corner, also by Roubiliac, is of the English Field Marshal Ligonier (?1763). On the wall next to the exit door are marble busts by the French sculptor Antoine Coysevox. They represent the French marshals Villars (1718) in the corner and Vauban (1706) by the door.

Above the chimney-piece is a painting by Pierre Mignard representing Princess Charlotte, Duchess of Orléans (great granddaughter of King James I) with her son Philip, the future Regent of France (dressed in girl's clothes, as was the custom) and her daughter Elizabeth, who was later to marry the Duc de Lorraine.

Above the exit door is a portrait by Edmund Lilly of Queen Anne's son William, Duke of Gloucester, who died in 1700 at the age of 11. The four armchairs against the fireplace wall are Italian, probably Genoese, *c.* 1700.

ABOVE: *Marble bust of the composer George Frederick Handel whose music was played to King George III in these rooms.*

Receptions are held in this room for the Diplomatic Corps when they come to Windsor Castle to pay their respects to a visiting Head of State. The Knights of the Garter also use it as a robing room.

ABOVE: *The Emperor Charles V (1500–58) by the Italian sculptor Leone Leoni.*

RIGHT: *Early 17th-century Italian foot combat armour, presented to the future King Charles II by the Duke of Savoy.*

The Queen's Guard Chamber was created in the 1670s for King Charles II's consort, Queen Catherine of Braganza. The extension overlooking the Quadrangle was added in 1828.

In the 17th century it was used as a waiting room. All were admitted who were respectably dressed. The Yeoman of the Guard stood guard in this room. Something of its original appearance is conveyed by the trophies of arms arranged in geometric patterns, which recall similar displays on its walls in the 17th century. The showcases contain dress swords, broad swords and armour, much of which was collected by King George IV.

The large equestrian figure represents the King's Champion, a member of the Dymoke family, whose hereditary function was to ride into Westminster Hall, London, after the banquet which used to follow the Coronation of a King or Queen in Westminster Abbey. The Champion would throw down his gauntlet (*seen here in his right hand*) three times and challenge anyone to deny that the new Sovereign was the lawful heir to the throne. The Sovereign subsequently drank the health of the Champion, who would then back his horse out of the hall. The last Coronation at which this ceremony was performed was that of King George IV in 1821.

ABOVE: *Small sword, probably German, mid-18th century, set with over 1,000 diamonds. It was used at the Coronation of King George IV in 1821.*

ABOVE: *The Queen's Guard Chamber. Above the chimney-piece is an equestrian portrait of Frederick Prince of Wales, King George III's father, by Joachim Kayser.*

The suit of armour seen here was made in 1585 for Sir Christopher Hatton, Lord Chancellor to Queen Elizabeth I. It was given to the King's Champion following King James II's Coronation Banquet in April 1685.

On either side stand fine busts of Arthur, Duke of Wellington, and John, Duke of Marlborough, each surmounted by a standard, one bearing the French tricolor and the other the arms of the Kings of France. These are rendered annually by the present Dukes as token rents for their estates, Stratfield Saye and Blenheim Palace respectively, awarded to their ancestors for their victories over the French at the battles of Waterloo (1815) and Blenheim (1704).

It is in St George's Hall in June each year that Her Majesty and The Duke of Edinburgh and the other 24 Knights of the Order of the Garter assemble before walking in procession down to St George's Chapel for their annual service.

The Queen also uses the room for large formal banquets for visiting Heads of State. For those occasions a dining table runs virtually the whole length of the room and seats up to 160 guests. In addition Her Majesty uses the Hall for receptions, such as those for members of the Royal Victorian Order, the Order of Chivalry which is in Her Majesty's personal gift. Dinners, plays and concerts have been given here by Sovereigns over many centuries.

The western half of the Hall (*the entrance end*) formed the Sovereign's private chapel from the 13th century until the early 19th century. It had been rebuilt for King Charles II in an elaborate baroque style; but by the late 1820s this chapel was in such a decayed condition that it was demolished by Sir Jeffry Wyatville and made into the present single, large room by combining it with the eastern half (*far end*) of the Hall which was built by King Edward III in the 1360s as a dining hall for the original members of the Order of the Garter.

It is decorated with shields bearing the coats of arms of all the Knights of the Garter, from the foundation of the Order in 1348 to the present day. Two shields are blank, those of the Dukes of Monmouth and Ormonde. They were deprived of their knighthoods in 1688 and 1715 respectively, following their attempts to overthrow their Sovereigns.

Hanging on the walls are portraits of Kings and Queens, going back in time from King James I (1603–1625) (*on the left*) to King George IV (1820–1830) (*at the far end*). Above the canopy at the far (*east*) end of the Hall is an organ which can be played in both St George's Hall and in the private chapel to the east of the Hall, which was built for Queen Victoria by Edward Blore in 1843.

ABOVE: *Coats of arms of Knights of the Garter. The Duke of Ormonde's shield is blank; he was deprived of his Knighthood after the Jacobite rebellion in 1715.*

RIGHT: *The baroque chapel made for King Charles II in the 1670s; changed into the west end of the present St George's Hall (see page 43 opposite) in the 1820s.*

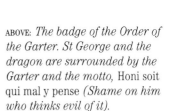

ABOVE: *The badge of the Order of the Garter. St George and the dragon are surrounded by the Garter and the motto,* Honi soit qui mal y pense *(Shame on him who thinks evil of it).*

RIGHT: *The Queen and other members of the Order of the Garter processing through St George's Hall on their way to St George's Chapel.*

On the right of the entrance is Roubiliac's lively representation of King George II and, to the left, Rysbrack's bust of the same monarch. On the left wall are busts of George III, George IV and William IV followed by two of Prince Albert, consort of Queen Victoria, and two of Victoria herself (at the age of 79 and 20 respectively. Along the window wall there are (*from right to left*) busts of George Duke of Cambridge followed by five of George III's six sons, Adolphus Duke of Cambridge, Frederick Duke of York, Ernest Duke of Cumberland, Augustus Duke of Sussex and Edward Duke of Kent. After them are busts of Queen Victoria's four sons, King Edward VII, Alfred Duke of Edinburgh, Arthur Duke of Connaught and Leopold Duke of Albany.

ABOVE: *St George's Hall looking west. A relief of St George, patron saint of the Order of the Garter, is above the west gallery.*

The Queen regularly uses this room for receptions before formal lunches or dinners held in the adjoining St George's Hall or in the Waterloo Chamber. The room was King Charles II's Guard Chamber. In the 1820s King George IV decided to transform it into a ballroom but it was not until early in the following reign that the work was completed.

ABOVE: *Ornamental musical instruments forming part of the ornate wall decorations added by Wyatville in the late 1820s.*

The panelling, with its richly gilded rococo decoration, is inspired by the French Louis XV style of the mid-18th century and is an early example of the English 19th-century revival of this style. The tapestries, which depict the story of Jason and the Golden Fleece, were woven at the Gobelins factory in France in the late 18th century; they were bought by King George IV in 1826.

Also French is a bronze reduction of a statue of King Louis XV (*left*) which was cast in 1776 and represents the King on a shield supported by four warriors. The unusual design recalls the custom of the Gauls, whose leaders, paraded on a shield, were elected by popular acclaim. The bronze busts represent (*on the left wall*) Cardinal Richelieu and King Charles I; and (*on the right*) the French Marshals, Condé and Turenne.

On the mantelpieces are an English clock and thermometer by Vulliamy in the Chinese style, dating from about 1820, which were originally in the Banqueting Room at Brighton Pavilion, King George IV's exotic marine residence of Indo-Chinese inspiration. The enormous mid 19th-century malachite vase in the window is Russian and was given to Queen Victoria by Tsar Nicholas I in 1839.

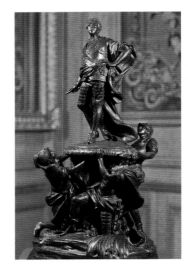

ABOVE: *Bronze statue of King Louis XV, 1776, by Jean-Baptiste [II] Lemoyne.*

LEFT: *Queen Victoria entertaining King Louis Philippe of France in the Grand Reception Room in 1844.*

RIGHT: *The Grand Reception Room, created in the late 1820s for King George IV by his architect, Sir Jeffry Wyatville.*

It is in this room that The Queen invests new Knights of the Order of the Garter before their installation. On the walls are portraits of Sovereigns in their Garter Robes from King George I to Queen Victoria. Hanging above the chimney-piece is the State Portrait of The Queen by Sir James Gunn painted in 1954.

Since the 12th century this room has been part of the Royal apartments. In the 1670s it formed two rooms, the division occurring two-thirds of the way down. The first part was King Charles II's Presence Chamber, and the second part, which included the space beyond now used as a separate room, the King's Audience Chamber. The room was converted by Wyatville during the reign of King George IV. The wall to which the canopy is attached was erected in the 1830s. The fine wood-carvings are by Grinling Gibbons and date from the late 17th century.

LEFT: *The Garter Throne Room, where Knights of the Garter assemble when The Queen invests new Knights. The State Portrait of The Queen (1954) hangs above the chimney-piece.*

The portraits of Queen Victoria and Prince Albert in Garter Robes are by Franz Xaver Winterhalter; and those of King George I and King George II (*on the wall to the left of the throne*) are by Sir Godfrey Kneller. On the left of the entrance is King George IV from the studio of Sir Thomas Lawrence and to his right his brother King William IV by Sir Martin Archer Shee.

ABOVE: *King George VI investing Princess Elizabeth with the Order of the Garter, 23 April 1948. On the left is Queen Elizabeth The Queen Mother.*

LEFT: *Model in marble and gilt bronze of the Arch of Constantine, Rome. The Prince Regent (later King George IV) bought this and two other models in 1816.*

It is in the Waterloo Chamber that The Queen lunches with the Knights of the Garter before their annual service in St George's Chapel. On this occasion, the magnificently laid table is set for 50 or 60 guests. The room is also the setting for concerts and plays, and for balls, as on the occasion when The Queen celebrated her 60th birthday.

During the Second World War all the paintings in the Castle were removed for safe storage. The Queen, then Princess Elizabeth, and Princess Margaret took part in Christmas pantomimes in this room. For these entertainments cartoon characters were painted in the blank spaces left by the missing paintings; some of these cartoons still survive behind the portraits.

Queen Victoria often used this room for formal dinners for visiting Heads of State, including Tsar Nicholas I of Russia in 1844 and the Emperor Napoleon III in 1855. On this last occasion it was tactfully and temporarily renamed the Music Room.

Although the plans for this room date from the 1820s, it was not completed until after King George IV's death in 1830. The room is built on the site of an open courtyard, known as Horn Court, so named after the two pairs of antlers of remarkable size with which it was hung.

The intention behind the creation of the Waterloo Chamber was to celebrate the victory of the Allies over Napoleon by hanging portraits of those leaders—Sovereigns, soldiers and statesmen—who had contributed most significantly to Napoleon's defeat. King George IV commissioned Sir Thomas Lawrence to paint the majority of the portraits. Perhaps the finest portrait is that of Pope Pius VII (*at the far end of the wall opposite the entrance*), who was a reluctant witness of Napoleon's coronation as Emperor in Paris in 1804.

On the right wall of the room are portraits of King George III (*over the chimney-piece*) with King George IV next to him on the right and King William IV (by Sir David Wilkie) to the left. On the opposite wall is the Emperor Francis I of Austria (*over the chimney-piece*) with Tsar Alexander I of Russia on the left and King Frederick William III of Prussia on the right. In the centre above the gallery (*on the left*) is the victor of Waterloo, the Duke of Wellington, with his Prussian ally Marshal Blücher on the right and his Russian ally Count Platoff, Hetman of the Cossacks, on the left. The Austrian Field Marshal, Prince Schwarzenberg, is opposite the Duke of Wellington above the west gallery (*far end*) with the Austrian Commander-in-Chief, the Archduke Charles, on the right and King Charles X of France on the left.

The seamless Indian carpet from Agra was presented to Queen Victoria in 1893 and is among the largest in existence. It measures 167 feet (51 m) long by 24 feet (7.5 m) wide.

ABOVE: *The Duke of Wellington, victor of the Battle of Waterloo, 1815. Painting by Sir Thomas Lawrence, commissioned by King George IV.*

RIGHT: *Ceiling of the Waterloo Chamber, completed in the 1830s; the chandeliers were added in 1862 and the skylights, by Willement, two years later.*

BELOW: *King George IV, who created the Waterloo Chamber to commemorate the Battle of Waterloo.*

RIGHT: *Queen Victoria leading King Louis Philippe of France into the Waterloo Chamber in 1844.*

FAR RIGHT: *The Queen seated (with her back to the chimney-piece) at lunch with Knights of the Order of the Garter before their annual service in St George's Chapel.*

At the time of a State Visit The Queen uses this room to introduce foreign Heads of State to The Prince and Princess of Wales and other members of the Royal Family.

This lofty chamber with its fine Gothic vaulting was designed as the landing for an earlier Grand Staircase, built for King George III in 1804 by James Wyatt (uncle of Sir Jeffry Wyatville). The most striking feature of Wyatt's work, the lantern and ceiling decorated with plasterwork by Bernasconi, survives.

The Gothic showcases, which were made in 1888 for the display of Queen Victoria's Golden Jubilee presents, now contain collections of European and Oriental arms and relics.

In the cabinet to the right of the entrance (*marked F*) are items associated with the Napoleonic Wars: Marshal Jourdan's baton and Joseph Bonaparte's sword captured at the Battle of Vitoria in 1813; an ivory-hilted sword (1799) which belonged to Napoleon when First Consul; a cloak presented to King George IV by Marshal Blücher, which the French Emperor reputedly wore on his Egyptian campaigns; and the bullet which killed Lord Nelson at the Battle of Trafalgar in 1805.

In the cabinet to the left of the entrance (*marked G*) are the robes worn by King George IV when he was crowned King of Hanover in 1821. The two marble busts are of King William III (*right*) and King Charles I (*left*).

In the far right-hand case (*marked P*) are trophies of Tipu Sultan, King of Mysore, which were seized when, in 1799, the British troops under the command of Major General George Harris stormed his capital, Seringapatam, and slew the Prince.

ABOVE: *Sword of Joseph Bonaparte (brother of Napoleon), King of Spain. Sent to the Prince Regent by the Duke of Wellington after the Battle of Vitoria, 1813.*

RIGHT: *Tiger's head of gold and rock crystal which used to support the dais of Tipu Sultan, King of Mysore. Captured by British troops, 1799.*

ABOVE: *Sword used by Napoleon Bonaparte when First Consul (1799–1804). Made in Versailles. Bought for the Royal Collection in 1827.*

RIGHT: *King George III's Grand Vestibule, 1804. A former Grand Staircase used to lead through the door, now blocked, behind Sir Edgar Boehm's statue (1871) of Queen Victoria.*

The Dolls' House was given to Queen Mary in 1924. It was designed by the celebrated architect Sir Edwin Lutyens and nearly every item in it was specially commissioned on the tiny scale of twelve to one. The mechanical and engineering equipment is made to work, including the water system, the electric lights and the two lifts. The gramophone plays and the bottles in the wine cellar contain genuine vintage wines.

The furniture and other contents were made by the leading manufacturers of the day. The paintings were commissioned from well-known artists and the books on the shelves of the library were written by prominent authors, some in their own hand. Rudyard Kipling, G. K. Chesterton, Sir Arthur Conan Doyle, Thomas Hardy and J. M. Barrie are among the writers represented.

On completion, the Dolls' House was shown at the British Empire Exhibition at Wembley, London, in 1924 and in the following year at the ninth Ideal Home Exhibition at Olympia, London. It was then installed in its present location, a former china store, which was adapted by Lutyens to its present use. Queen Mary directed that the entrance fees should go to charities, as they still do today.

BELOW: *The Library of the Dolls' House. The tiny books were specially written by famous authors of the early 1920s. The cabinets to right and left contain minute watercolours by prominent artists.*

BOTTOM: *The Entrance Hall of the Dolls' House.*

BELOW: *The newly completed Dolls' House in 1924 in the Drawing Room of the London house of Sir Edwin Lutyens, the designer of the Dolls' House. It is being packed up before going on exhibition at Wembley.*

The Exhibition of The Queen's Presents and Royal Carriages shows some of the items associated with the Royal Family's interest in horses, including a selection of historic coaches and carriages. Also included is a display of interesting and exotic gifts which have been presented to Her Majesty in recent years.

The area where the Exhibition is held is in St Albans Street next to Burford House, which is occupied by staff of the Royal Mews. The house was originally built in the 1670s by King Charles II for one of his mistresses, Nell Gwynn.

In the Royal Mews (*not open to the public*), which is the area behind the exhibition rooms, are kept some of the horses (including polo ponies), carriages and cars belonging to The Queen, The Duke of Edinburgh and The Prince of Wales.

The stables in the Mews include a large indoor riding school, which was completed in 1842, and the Castle's own fire station.

ABOVE: *A pair of miniature heads presented to The Queen by the Governor and people of Ayuddhaya, Thailand, in 1972.*

ABOVE: *Queen Victoria's Royal Arms surrounded by her Garter Collar depicted on the box seat cover of the State Landau.*

LEFT: *Queen Victoria and the French King, Louis Philippe, in a charabanc which he had presented to her during his State visit to Windsor in 1844.*

LEFT: *The same charabanc standing outside the Mews exhibition, where it can be seen today. In front of it is the Scottish State Coach, still used by The Queen on special occasions.*

THE NORMANS

THE EARLY PLANTAGENETS

KING WILLIAM I (1066–1087)

KING HENRY II (1154–1189)

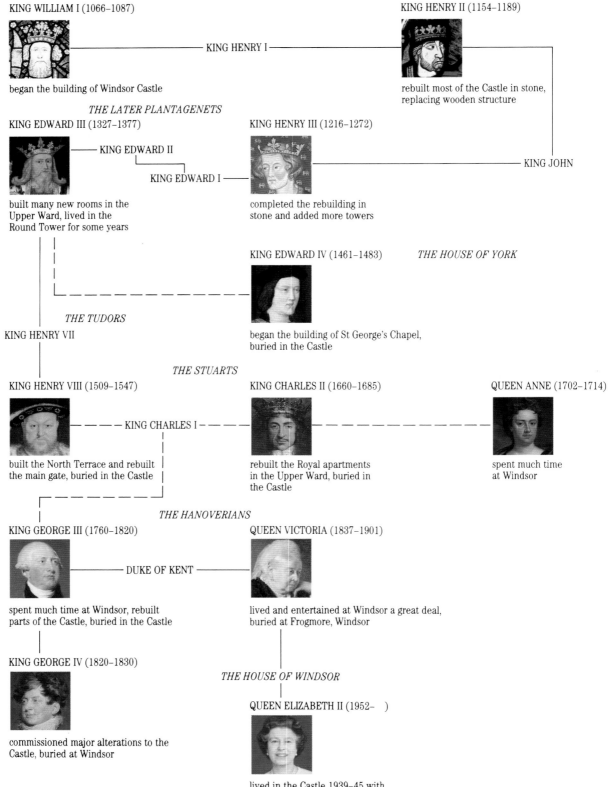

KING HENRY I

began the building of Windsor Castle

rebuilt most of the Castle in stone, replacing wooden structure

THE LATER PLANTAGENETS

KING EDWARD III (1327–1377)

KING EDWARD II

KING EDWARD I

KING HENRY III (1216–1272)

KING JOHN

built many new rooms in the Upper Ward, lived in the Round Tower for some years

completed the rebuilding in stone and added more towers

KING EDWARD IV (1461–1483)

THE HOUSE OF YORK

THE TUDORS

KING HENRY VII

began the building of St George's Chapel, buried in the Castle

THE STUARTS

KING HENRY VIII (1509–1547)

KING CHARLES I

KING CHARLES II (1660–1685)

QUEEN ANNE (1702–1714)

built the North Terrace and rebuilt the main gate, buried in the Castle

rebuilt the Royal apartments in the Upper Ward, buried in the Castle

spent much time at Windsor

THE HANOVERIANS

KING GEORGE III (1760–1820)

DUKE OF KENT

QUEEN VICTORIA (1837–1901)

spent much time at Windsor, rebuilt parts of the Castle, buried in the Castle

lived and entertained at Windsor a great deal, buried at Frogmore, Windsor

KING GEORGE IV (1820–1830)

THE HOUSE OF WINDSOR

QUEEN ELIZABETH II (1952–   )

commissioned major alterations to the Castle, buried at Windsor

lived in the Castle 1939–45 with Princess Margaret, spends many weekends at Windsor as well as Easter, Christmas and Ascot week

1070 WILLIAM I. Construction in earth and timber begun of a central fortress and perimeter ramparts.

1170s HENRY II. Castle largely rebuilt in stone with square towers introduced in the perimeter wall. Improvements made to living quarters in Upper Ward.

1220s HENRY III. West wall of Castle rebuilt in stone and five rounded towers added to perimeter walls.

1240–48 HENRY III. Chapel built (since replaced) on site of present Albert Memorial Chapel.

1358–68 EDWARD III. In Upper Ward range of apartments added along south and east walls. Royal apartments in north range extended, which included the building of St George's Hall (1362–65); Norman Tower and Gate built. In Lower Ward Deanery, Canons' residences and upper range of Military Knights' houses built.

1475–1528 EDWARD IV, HENRY VII, HENRY VIII. St George's Chapel built.

1511 HENRY VIII. In Lower Ward King Henry VIII Gate replaced that of Henry III.

1550s MARY I. In Lower Ward lower range of Military Knights' houses built.

1583 ELIZABETH I. In Upper Ward Queen Elizabeth's Gallery built.

1675–83 CHARLES II. Royal apartments extensively remodelled and built in part (Star Building). Architect Hugh May. Long Walk laid out.

1823–32 GEORGE IV, WILLIAM IV. Round Tower heightened by 30 feet (9.1 m), the buildings generally Gothicised, refaced and heightened with battlements, turrets and towers added. In Upper Ward apartments in south and east ranges remodelled and Grand Corridor added. Long Walk extended into Quadrangle. In State Apartments in north range, alterations begun in 1820s and completed in 1830s. Architect Sir Jeffry Wyatville.

1866–67 QUEEN VICTORIA. Existing Grand Staircase built. Architect Anthony Salvin.

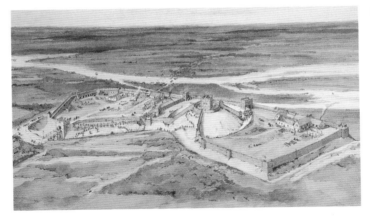

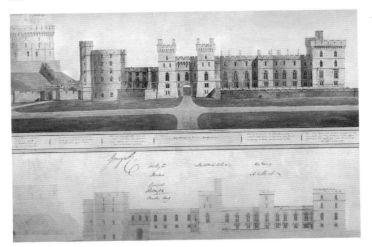

LEFT: Reconstruction of Windsor Castle in its original 'motte and bailey' form about 1070. An artificial mound of earth, the 'motte', was surrounded by wooden defences and encircled by a ditch. Beyond the ditch lay the bailey, a wide, level area bordered with similar defences and protected by an outer earthen rampart. The ditches were filled with water where the lie of the land permitted. This view is looking from the south.

ABOVE: Bird's-eye view of Windsor Castle from the north, made for King James I by John Norden in 1607. In the left foreground stand the 14th-century Royal apartments of King Edward III, with King Henry VII's building and Queen Elizabeth's Gallery on their right. Between them and the Round Tower is a tennis court. The fountain in the middle of the Quadrangle provided the water supply. In the right foreground stands St George's Chapel.

ABOVE: *The south front of the Upper Ward before (below) and after (above) its remodelling for King George IV by Sir Jeffry Wyatville in the 1820s. The Round Tower, on the left, was raised by 30 feet (9.1m) with a battlement rising above the coping. The new St George's Gate, seen below the Round Tower, was made as an entrance to the south-west corner of the Quadrangle. The foundation stone of the new King George IV Gate, in the centre, was laid by the King on 12 August 1824. Lancaster Tower, on the left of the arch, was new; York Tower, on the right, was an old tower raised and altered. The south range of the Royal apartments were made a storey higher. New stone windows and mullions were added to the Queen's Tower on the far right-hand side. The drawings bear King George IV's signature approving the plans.*

The Great Park, comprising some 5,700 acres (2,280 ha), is connected to Windsor Castle by the Long Walk, a straight avenue of trees running for nearly three miles (4.8km) due south from the Castle (King George IV Gate) to the 'Copper Horse', an equestrian statue of King George III by Sir Richard Westmacott, situated on Snow Hill and erected in 1831.

During Ascot week The Queen and her guests drive by car each day down the Long Walk. Then they change from cars to horse-drawn landaus in the Great Park before driving to the Ascot racecourse.

The Long Walk was originally planted by King Charles II in the 1680s with two double rows of elm trees. They eventually became diseased and were replaced in 1945 by the present rows of London planes and horse chestnuts. (*The Long Walk is open to the public on foot except for the short section nearest the Castle.*)

The Great Park is run by the Ranger, The Duke of Edinburgh, a Deputy Ranger, the Crown Estate Commissioners and staff. The arable land within the Great Park forms a part of the Royal Farms farmed by Her Majesty and covers an area of about 1,200 acres (480 ha). Part of the park is stocked with a herd of red deer which can often be seen from the Long Walk. Within the park stands Royal Lodge, a residence of Queen Elizabeth The Queen Mother (*not open to the public*).

The Prince of Wales often plays polo in the summer at the Guard's Polo Club, Smith's Lawn (*open to the public*). The Duke of Edinburgh also used to play polo there and still uses the Home Park and Great Park in which to drive his horses and carriages in practice and in competitions.

Close to Smith's Lawn are the Savill and Valley Gardens, created in 1932 and 1949 respectively, wonderful examples of landscape gardening (*open to the public throughout the year*).

RIGHT: *The south front of Windsor Castle, view from The Long Walk.*